Island Women

*Photographs of East End Women
1897 to 1983*

Eve Hostettler

NiSHEN PHOTOGRAPHY

Island Women

Photographs of East End Women 1897 to 1983

The photographs in this book have been selected from the Photograph Collection of the Island History Trust, a community history project on the Isle of Dogs in East London. All the women featured in the book, or their descendants, have lived, or still live, in either Millwall or Cubitt Town, the two districts of the Island.

The Isle of Dogs is part of the London Borough of Tower Hamlets, and is close to the City of London, but as its name suggests, it is relatively isolated from the rest of the capital by its geographical situation in a loop of the River Thames. The Island was uninhabited marshland until the West India Docks were built here in 1802. Shipyards and related trades were established soon afterwards along the western embankment, attracting industrial workers from all over the country. In the 1860s, the Millwall Docks were opened and during the later part of the nineteenth century, as ship-building declined, other industries – mechanical engineering, metal-working, oil and chemical processing, packaging, food processing – grew and prospered. These firms, and the docks, provided a range of jobs which brought more and more people to live on the Island, even though much of the work was casual and poorly paid. By 1900 a close-knit working-class community of 21000 people was established here.

The docks are now closed to trade, and the industries have gone; but in spite of this industrial decline, and the earlier upheavals of the Second World War, a community spirit still flourishes amidst the modern office blocks and private housing estates which are being built in the 1980s, as part of a redevelopment programme. The Island History Trust was established in 1980 with the aim of recovering and preserving the history of the Isle of Dogs and the people who live here; the Trust now has the active support of hundreds of Islanders. A product of that support is the Photograph Collection. This consists of some 3000 prints, made from copy negatives of originals loaned by Islanders – originals which have been preserved for years in albums, biscuit tins and faded envelopes, and which are now being brought together to form a public archive.

The Collection reflects the social history of photography as well as of the community. Some of the best quality pictures, for clarity of reproduction, are the formal studio portraits of the early twentieth century. These were often bought through Photograph Clubs, which existed in many workplaces. The nature of the Island's economy was such that everyone in the family had to start work as soon as they could leave school; many women continued to work after marriage. Island girls and women were employed in the local factories: they sewed tarpaulins, wound ropes, processed and packed a variety of foodstuffs, made sacks, boxes and packing cases, tested cables and shovelled chemicals into vats; they also served in bars, canteens and coffee shops and worked in offices. For the special occasion of having their studio portrait taken, they abandoned their working clothes and appeared in their formal best.

The work of the professional photographer is visible in the many group photographs in the Collection, which illustrate the neighbourhood and kinship networks of the community – networks which provided women with

THE ANNUAL WOMEN'S OUTING

The annual women's outing from *The Tooke Arms* public house, Millwall, in 1922. Mrs Florence Vincent (*née* Eaton), recalls: 'The outing took place every summer. There would always be plenty of children hanging around, because, as the coach started off, pennies were thrown and us kids would scramble for them. My eldest sister was in charge of us and we knew that we would have a stick of rock each the next morning. It was the only day out my mum had.'

Front cover and title page

A class of Island schoolgirls at St John's Church of England School, Cubitt Town. The teacher is Miss Rose Sole; in front on the left is Lilian Daisy Ward (b.1888), who became a dressmaker when she left school. Some of the girls are wearing the medals which they were given for good attendance; Lilian's medal, which is still in the family, is dated '1897'.

much comfort and support in the face of poverty. Photographers also went from house to house to find business. Mothers gathered together and tidied up their children, and the resulting prints are treasured now, often as the only record of a grandmother or a great-aunt. With the wide availability of the cheap portable camera in the 1920s, some Islanders became avid amateur photographers and have preserved dozens of snaps. If the quality is less uniformly good in these pictures than in the professional photographs, the record is more complete. The camera was taken on holiday to the seaside, down to the hop-fields of Kent, into the back yard or garden and was smuggled into the work-place; a visual history of everyday life on the Island, before and after the Second World War, came into being.

War-time restrictions on photography are reflected in the scant coverage of the years 1939–1945 in the Collection. Perhaps few local people would have cared to record the destruction caused by the Blitz. The photographs which do exist not only provide sorrowful reflections, but also a pride, tinged with regret, in the skilled work and responsibilities which women undertook for the duration of the war.

In general, the use of the personal camera to record the happy moment, to preserve the pleasant memory, is apparent throughout the Collection. There are no amateur photographs illustrating the ill-health, or the care of the sick and frail, which have been, and remain, central to the lives of working-class women. The two photographs of sick-beds reproduced here are professional pictures, taken with the knowledge of approaching death.

In many material ways, the lives of Island women have greatly improved during this century. The hard, heavy, low-paid factory work has gone; educational and job opportunities have widened somewhat – though there is still unemployment and poverty. For many, life has become more comfortable – and more private. Homes no longer have to be shared with relatives and lodgers; annual outings and hop-picking have lost their appeal in the face of the foreign holiday and the motor car. Photographs too, have lost some of their magic. From the 1970s, mass production and keen marketing by the photographic industry have ensured that almost every household has in its possession at least one camera, loaded with colour film. Modern photographs are regarded as so commonplace that little social or historic value is attached to them and they are rarely offered to the Collection. A contemporary photographic project was organized by the Trust in the 1980s in order to record the events of this period and to ensure that the Collection continues to grow and to reflect the changing life of the community.

Eve Hostettler

Daisy Thomas (*later* Clayden), b.1901. 'This was taken about 1916 – because I was wearing black for my grandfather. I was working at Venesta's then, and I used to belong to a Photograph Club at the factory; you'd pay a penny a week, and when your turn came up, you'd go and have your photograph done. I had that taken at Whiffin's, in East India Dock Road.'

Sarah Jane Morris (*née* Bell), b.1862 in Norfolk, d.1921. Sarah and her husband, a stevedore, had seven children. In this photograph she is wearing a black sateen blouse, made from the lining of a man's jacket. She is in mourning for her son John William, who was killed in action in 1917.

Mary Ann Wright (*née* Newbury), b.1895 in Limehouse, d.1977. Mary was a barmaid in the *North Pole* public house on the Isle of Dogs and during the First World War she worked as a welder. She married a docker and they had a family of nine boys and two girls, though one girl died as a baby. All Mary's sons grew up to be dockers, stevedores or welders and many of her descendants still live on the Isle of Dogs.

Susan Archbold (*later* Hawkins), b.1889, with her fiancé Joe, in 1909. Joe played for Millwall Football Club in his youth, and Susan remained a lifelong supporter of the team, going all over the country to watch them play. She had two children and did not work after marriage as Joe had a regular, well-paid job as a chief tally clerk with a stevedoring firm in the docks.

Catherine Mary Ann Studd (*née* Ellis), b.1858 in Essex, d.1947. Catherine worked as a maidservant in The Hall at Kirby-le-Soken and in 1883 she married George Studd, a sailor, of that village. He worked on ships trading out of the Millwall Docks and so the couple moved to the Isle of Dogs. This photograph was taken in the 1930s at the door of their home in Cahir Street.

Eunice Walsh (*née* French), b.1913. At the time of her marriage to John Walsh of Deptford, in 1931, Eunice's parents were caretakers at Samuel Cutler's steel works; the wedding ceremony took place in St Edmund's Roman Catholic Church, across the road from the steel works. This photograph was taken on the riverside, in front of the works canteen, where the wedding reception was held.

Rose May Earle (*née* Gibson), b.1886, d.1949. Rose worked as a house-parlourmaid for a Member of Parliament in Eaton Square, Central London. After her marriage she worked as cook in a local factory. She had two children and is pictured here with the elder, John, in 1910.

LOUISE STANLEY

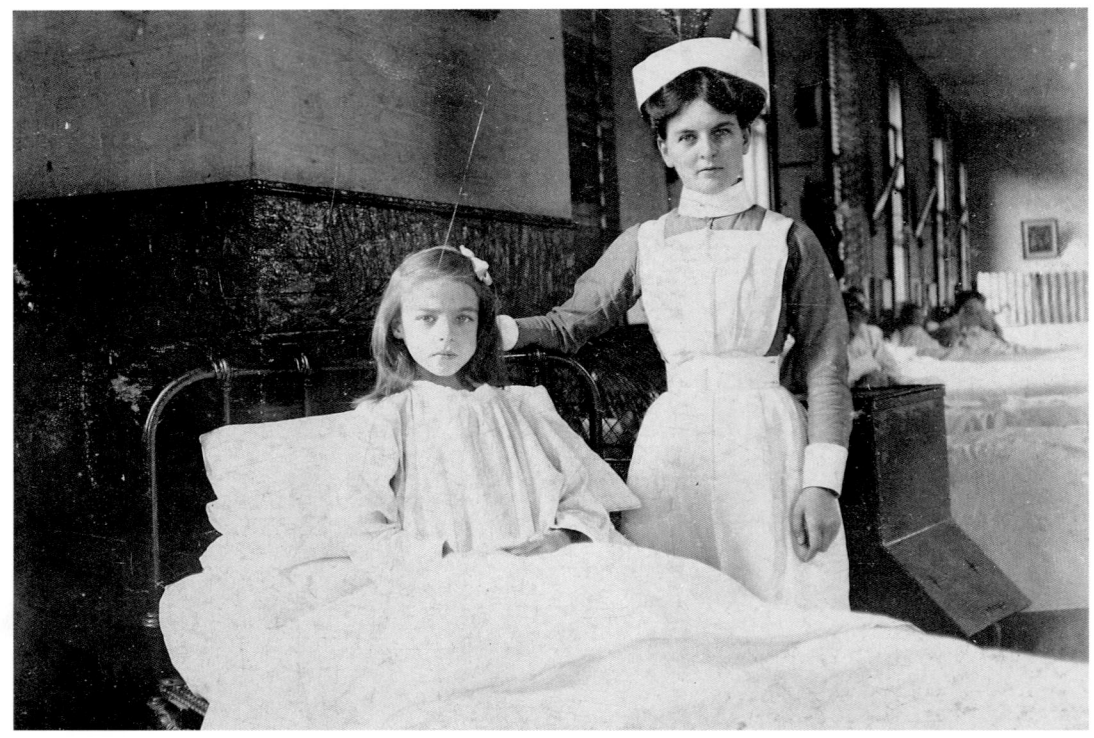

Louise Stanley, b.1887, in Stepney. Louise was always in and out of hospital from the day she was born. This photograph, with the ward sister, was taken in Mile End Hospital, in Bancroft Road, in 1902. Louise, who was the eldest of 13 children, died two weeks after the photograph was taken, from a combination of diseases including tuberculosis.

Margaret Elizabeth Maxwell (*née* Rispin), b.1885 in Yorkshire. Margaret suffered from rheumatoid arthritis, and could not walk because of her ulcerated legs; she was cared for at home by her daughter, the eldest of her four children. She had a sofa in the back yard of her home in Harrap Street, Poplar, where this photograph was taken in June 1930. She died three months later.

ANNIE ETHEL FRENCH

Annie Ethel French, b.1890, d.1945, with her family in 1923. Her son Alfred recalls: 'My mother worked from morning till night as most mothers did in those days. I was away on active service but I saw her two years before she died and she was an old lady; grey hair, her face was lined, her hands were roughened with constant washing and scrubbing and brushing and hauling shopping.'

Nora Dutfield (*née* Bradley), b.1890, pictured with her family in 1927. In the photograph are: Eileen, b.1915; baby Lily, b.1927; Nora's husband Harry with the dog Peter; Nora, b.1916; Kathleen, b.1919; Beatrice, b.1925; Tommy, b.1922; and Mary, b.1918. The family lived in a six-roomed house in West Ferry Road.

Members of the Clayden family, hop-picking in Kent in 1925. 'It was hard work, let me tell you! Of course, you're standing up all day, from seven in the morning until six at night, with an hour's break for dinner. When I came home, I used to buy the children new boots to go back to school, and the rest went in the Post Office.'

THE HOP-PICKERS' HUT

Mary Ann Wright outside her 'hopping hut' in Kent in the 1950s. These huts were equipped with a large wooden bunk bed; straw was provided, and some hoppers took their feather mattresses with them. Other household goods were carried in a tea chest; emptied and turned upside down, this made an indoor table. Cooking was done outside over open fires if the weather was fine.

Workers from the confectionery department of C & E Morton's Millwall factory, out on strike in the 1930s over the sacking of their foreman by a new manager. 'We were out for a fortnight, getting no money, as we weren't in a union then. In the end the manager had to have us all back, because no one else had the experience to set up our machines.'

An outing from *The Prince* public house, in Stewart Street, in the 1930s. 'It was a good old pub, right on the waterfront. Most of the women in the picture lived within a stone's throw of the pub. They paid a shilling or sixpence a week into a club and the outing was organised by the landlady, Mrs Smythe. We went to Margate or Southend for a day by the sea.'

Daisy Roberts (*later* Woodard), b.1927, with her grandmother, Daisy Kemp (*née* Still), b.1865, d.1941, photographed in the back yard of their home in Newcastle Street in 1938. Daisy's home was shared with several of her aunts and uncles and cousins as well as by her parents and grandparents. She recalls: 'My mum idolised her mum – same as I did – but they used to get on each other's nerves occasionally!'

Edith Jessie Binns (*née* Shaw) with her only daughter Betty Frances, b.1926, photographed in the garden of their home in Manchester Road. Edith worked in Venesta's plywood factory before she married Charles, a boiler-maker. Betty became a secretary and later married and had two children. When she was expecting her second child she was diagnosed as having a fatal disease and she died in 1961.

Rosie Bell (*now* Abbott), b.1919, with her boy-friend, Jim Gordon, and his parents, in 1937. Rosie worked in the Land Army until she married Jim in 1942; she then became a telephonist until her son was born. Jim, who was engaged in secret work with the Coastal Forces, was killed soon after VE day, shortly before the baby's birth.

Olive Hook (*later* Campbell), with two friends at Millwall Fire Station in 1939. 'We all joined up nine months before war broke out. We were at the hairdressers, and we decided on the toss of a coin to join the AFS. We were trained to read maps, and to mobilise the fire appliances; during the worst of the Blitz we were on duty more or less continuously.'

Elizabeth Reading, b.1870, d.1960, photographed in the garden of her home in Strattondale Street in the 1950s. Elizabeth, who is remembered as being: 'A Victorian through and through' is said to have been a money-lender. Money-lenders, who were usually women, were resorted to for major expenses, such as equipping children with new clothes for Procession Day, or for Christmas.

Martha Fitzearle (*née* White), b.1907, d.1969. Martha worked at McDougalls Flour Mill after leaving school. She married a barge builder and had three children. This photograph was taken in 1953, outside the prefabricated house in which the family was rehoused during the Blitz. Martha is remembered as being: 'A marvellous manager. She knitted, repaired shoes and made new clothes out of old. And she was a lovely cook.'

Christmas dinner in the works canteen at C & E Morton's Millwall factory in the 1950s. This firm employed many local women and their solidarity in the work-place reflected the family and neighbourhood relationships of the streets where they lived around the factory. The company was taken over by Beechams Foods in the 1950s and closed down in 1982, to be replaced by a private housing site.

Office workers at Rye Arc Limited, one of the last two remaining ship-repair firms on the Isle of Dogs in the 1960s. The world of work within the dock walls was predominantly, but not entirely, male; women were recruited for war work in the docks, and also worked as stewardesses on passenger liners, as ships' cleaners and in office administration.

Dolly Morris and Daisy Woodard (*née* Roberts) at Hawkins & Tipsons rope-works in 1954. Daisy recalls: 'We worked from eight till five or six o'clock, and Saturdays from eight till twelve. We got three pounds a week for that. That's my knife on a bit of string – you always had to have a sharp knife so that you could cut the rope quickly if anything went wrong.'

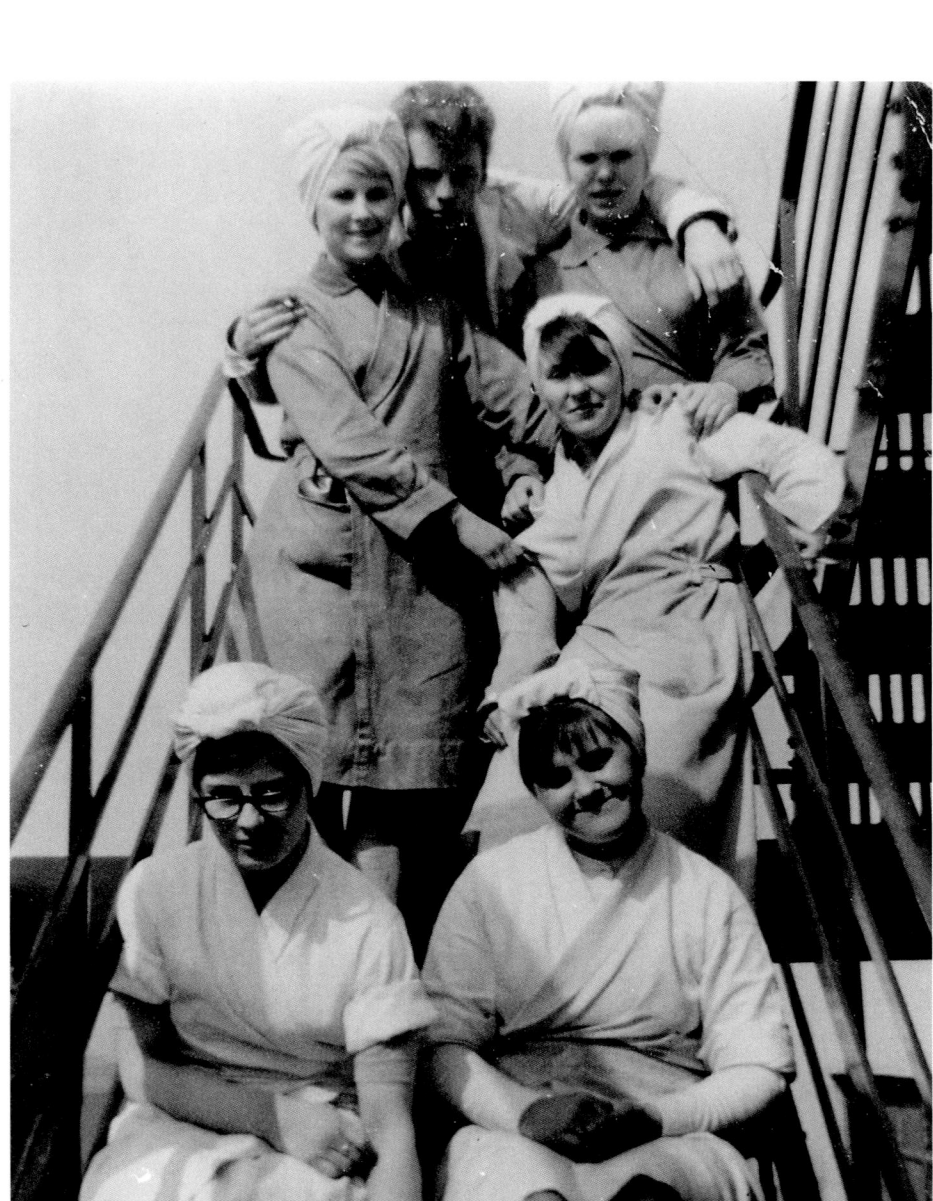

Mill workers at McDougalls Flour Mill, Millwall Docks, in the 1960s. This firm employed up to one hundred women in the packing department, on the stacking floor, in the works canteen and in the offices. The mill closed in 1981 but the tall white silos remained, visible for miles around, until they were demolished in 1985.

30 ■ A COMMUNITY MEETING

Members of the Association of Island Communities (the AIC) at a community meeting in 1983. The AIC, a federation of Island organisations, has its roots in the strong tenants' committees and other local groups established during the post-war period. Islanders' views on current issues are channelled through the AIC to the Borough Council and other policy-making bodies.

Two colour-makers in the works canteen at Blythe Burrell Colours Limited, Millwall, in 1983. The manufacture of pure colour in the largely unmodernized plant was heavy work – and wet work! 'Walking on concrete all day in Wellington boots really makes your feet ache – but you have to wear them. I finish the work and I scrub down for the day and I say: "Thank God! It's over"! The colour works closed down in 1986. *(Photograph by Mike Seaborne)*

ACKNOWLEDGEMENTS

The photographs and information have been provided by Islanders, and the editor would like to thank the following: Mrs Florence Vincent, Mrs Daisy Clayden, Mrs May Power, Joe Wright, Mrs Joan Horton, Jim Studd, Mrs Eileen Bannister, Mrs Ivy Hames, Ms Christine Egglesfield, Mrs Ettie Long, Mrs Wootley, Mrs Beatrice Payne, Alfred French, Mrs L Perfect, Mrs Lil Devonshire, Mrs Daisy Woodard, John Needham, Mrs Phillips, Reg Copland, Mrs Rose Abbott, Mrs Olive Campbell, Mrs Buddy Penn, Mrs Reading, Mrs Taylor, Mrs C Ezekiel, Miss L Hiscott, and workers at Blythe Burrell Colours Limited.

The pictures in this booklet are from the Island History Trust Collection. New prints were made from copy negatives taken from the original prints.

The publisher would like to thank: Eve Hostettler, for compiling this booklet; the Island History Trust for allowing access to the Collection; and all the other people who have assisted in the production.

Dirk Nishen will be pleased to send you further information about the Photo Library and a copy of his current catalogue

© Copyright Dirk Nishen Publishing
Text, captions and photographs copyright the Island History Trust
All rights reserved
Set in Berthold Poppl Pontifex regular
Phototypesetting   Nagel Fototype, D-Berlin
Origination   ORT Kirchner + Graser, D-Berlin
Printing   H Heenemann, D-Berlin
Binding   H Hensch, D-Berlin
Printed in Germany

ISBN 1 85378 105 3

Dirk Nishen Publishing
19 Doughty Street   London
WC1N 2PT   Great Britain
01 242 0185